BOLD KIDS

Ancient Inca

AMAZING AND INTRIGUING FACTS
CHILDREN'S HISTORY BOOK

For those interested in the culture of ancient Peru, these ancient Inca facts are sure to impress. These facts include information about the Inca emperor, religion, government, and technology. To learn more about these fascinating people, continue reading!

Ancient Inca facts reveal what people actually did and believed. These people used their skills to build large cities, paved the way for civilization, and even invented a sophisticated form of paper. Find out more in this book!

INCA EMPEROR VIRACOCHA

Viracocha was the eighth Sapa Inca, and emperor of Tawantinsuyu. His name meant "a god who creates" in Quechua. He also created the universe, including the sun, moon, stars, and time. He was considered to be the creator god and father of the Inca gods.

He taught humanity all of the necessary skills to become civilized, and then disappeared. The human race was then cared for by lesser gods. Viracocha's role in creating the world was to watch over his children and see if they were progressing.

The Incas called Viracocha, the supreme pan-Andean creator god, by several different names. In addition to his name, Viracocha's function may have referred to a lake, sea-fat, or foam.

Other Inca names for him include Ilya, Wiraqoca, and Pacayacaciq. The actual name of the Inca emperor was too sacred to mention, so he was often referred to as an Inca god.

The Incas began to expand their empire during the reign of Mayta Capac. Viracocha, with the help of his two uncles, ruled over the Urubamba Valley and the southern Ayarmaca kingdom.

In this period, the Incas developed their practice of leaving military garrisons in conquered lands. It was only in Viracocha's reign that the Inca empire truly became a world power.

INCA GOVERNMENT

The Ancient Inca government was a combination of monarchy, theocracy, and agrarian collectivism organized around a bureaucratic state. In ancient times, the Inca king was treated as a divine being.

The Sapa Inca was the supreme ruler and was believed to be a descendant of the sun god. The Sapa Inca was followed by Apos, who were the provincial governors of each part of the empire. These emperors had special powers and responsibilities, including taxes and labor, and they were able to appoint curacas.

The Ancient Inca government was divided into groups of ten nobles known as panqa. These groups were closely related to the emperor and held power through familial ties. They would advise the emperor and vote on who should become heir to the throne.

These groups often clashed with each other and sometimes open wars would break out. The hierarchy of power within the Inca government was complex, and rivalry among the panqa was intense.

The Inca empire also had a robust trade market. In order to maintain control over these markets, the government organized a highly structured administrative system.

This included a system of ayllu, which consisted of related individuals exchanging labor. Ayllu members also cooperated in the management of land, herds, and water resources. These ayllu's were named after the founding fathers of the society.

INCA RELIGION

Among the many fascinating Inca facts and religion, the idea of an afterlife was highly significant to the Inca culture. The dead emperors were mummified and guarded by servants during the festivals.

Their menstrual cycles were calculated using the waxing and waning of the moon, and silver was considered a tear of the moon. They also believed that the constellations Lyra and Scorpio were shaped like llamas, and the Pleiades were "little mothers." The Earth itself was considered the Pachamama, and all physical specimens lived within its boundaries.

In addition to the Sun God, the Incas worshipped a sun god called Virachoa. This god was the center of the institutional organization of society.

All life was centred on the Sun. Virachoa, also known as Apu Qun Tiqsi Wiraqutra, was considered the creator of civilization. He was worshipped through sacrifices. These sacrifices were meant to appease the gods of the sky and earth. The Moon and Earth were regarded as fertility, and humans were sacrificed to appease them.

The second-most important festival of the Incas was Inti Raymi, which took place in June. It was an eight to nine-day festival to celebrate the Sun god and to signal the beginning of the plowing season.

The feasts that followed were elaborate and often included sacrifices of white llamas. As the first emperor, Pachacuti made Cuzco into a great city in the shape of a puma, and installed Inti as its official patron.

INCA TECHNOLOGY

The ancient Incas used a complex calendar to keep track of time. Each calendar month was associated with a religious festival. There were 12 months, three weeks, and ten days in each week. The calendar was maintained by time makers, towers that measured time with the sun's position.

These towers would then add days to the calendar as necessary. Throughout the empire, this calendar was used to determine when the next major religious celebration would occur.

The Incas didn't use written language, but their mathematics was almost identical to the modern system. The Incas paid taxes in food, precious metals, textiles, and vicuna wool, a super-soft wool found only on the Incas' mountain tops.

In exchange for these valuable materials, the Incas produced beautiful ceramics. The most popular ceramic vessel was the urpu, a bulbous vessel for maize. Incas had complex agricultural systems, and divided land into three parts.

Many researchers now believe that the Incas also created the first agricultural systems in South America. They also cultivated and rehabilitated a variety of crops. They also used stone a variety of angles and heights to construct the most efficient water retention systems and structures.

This same method is currently being used to create freeze-dried food that astronauts consume every day. It's also possible that the Incas used a similar method to make their own canned goods.

INCA ARCHITECTURE

The Incas were famous for their attention to aesthetics, efficiency, and practicality. Their architecture is well-preserved in the Inca ruins at Machu Picchu, one of the seven wonders of the world.

Without the skillful Inca engineers, the city of Machu Picchu would have collapsed from the mountain. Nevertheless, the Incas left the city standing and it became a world-famous tourist destination.

Although many of the buildings in Machu Picchu were single-story, some included an attic or were built with curved walls. Despite the curved form of these buildings, their roofs would have been steeper than 60 degrees.

The drainage system of Inca towns was impeccable. Instead of having square blocks, the buildings were set parallel to the central plaza. The main roads in the towns were parallel to the plaza, and buildings were never square.

CPSIA information can be obtained
at www.ICGtesting.com
Printed in the USA
LVHW071604161222
735372LV00007B/250

9 781071 718735